POLITICAL PARTIES

BY M. WEBER

Fitchburg Public Library
5530 Lacy Road
Fitchburg, WI 53711

Published by The Child's World®
1980 Lookout Drive • Mankato, MN 56003-1705
800-599-READ • www.childsworld.com

PHOTO CREDITS
Shutterstock/vectorfusionart, cover, 2; Wikimedia/Mead Art Museum, 5 (top); Wikimedia/Ralph Eleazer Whiteside Earl, 5 (bottom); Wikimedia/Benjamin Franklin, 7; Wikimedia/Currier and Ives, 8; Getty Images/RobinOlimb, 11; Wikimedia/Thomas Nast, 12; Wikimedia/Social Security History, 14; Getty Images/studiogstock, 17; Wikimedia/FDR Presidential Library & Museum/Leon A. Perskie, 19; Wikimedia/Qqqqqq, 21

COPYRIGHT © 2021 by The Child's World®
All rights reserved. No part of this book may be reproduced or utilized in any form or by any means without written permission from the publisher.

ISBN 9781503844988 (REINFORCED LIBRARY BINDING)
ISBN 9781503846357 (PORTABLE DOCUMENT FORMAT)
ISBN 9781503847545 (ONLINE MULTI-USER EBOOK)
LCCN: 2019956596

Printed in the United States of America

On the cover: There are two main political parties in the United States.

TABLE OF CONTENTS

CHAPTER 1
What Political Parties Do...4

CHAPTER 2
History of the Republican Party...10

CHAPTER 3
History of the Democratic Party...16

GLOSSARY...22
TO LEARN MORE...23
INDEX...24
ABOUT THE AUTHOR...24

CHAPTER 1

WHAT POLITICAL PARTIES DO

Political parties are groups. They are made up of politicians and voters. The people in a political party agree on ideas. Political parties do many things. They help people run for office. Someone who runs for office is called a politician. They try to be elected, or voted into office. This is one of the main jobs of political parties. They also tell voters about issues. Political parties work together to solve problems. Voters choose **candidates** from political parties. The candidates and voters often agree on solutions.

Political parties are a part of every democratic government. That means people can vote for their leaders.

THIRD PARTIES

Every president in US history except for George Washington has belonged to a major political party. Ross Perot ran for president as an **Independent**. He ran in 1992. Perot won 19 percent of the vote. He is the only candidate to win that much support in a national election against the Democrats and Republicans.

FIRST OFFICIAL PARTY PRESIDENTS

Abraham Lincoln, first Republican president

Andrew Jackson, first Democratic president

Some countries have many political parties. The United States has two main groups. This is a called a two-party system. The two main parties are the Republicans and the Democrats. There are some smaller political parties. One of these parties is the Independent party. Most people vote for either a Republican or Democrat. It is rare to have someone win from a third party.

Political parties started soon after the country was founded. The US government formed after the Revolutionary War (1775–1783). The United States won independence from Great Britain. Then a group of leaders called the Founding Fathers created a new government. The first two parties were the Federalists and the Anti-Federalists. The Federalists wanted to **ratify** the US Constitution. The Constitution was written to guide the new government. The Anti-Federalists did not like the Constitution. They argued against it. Political parties often take opposite views on big issues. This has been true since the country began.

The Democrats and the Republicans do not agree on many issues today. People decide to join a party based on their beliefs. But the job of both political parties is the same.

Benjamin Franklin created the first American political cartoon. He was trying to convince the American colonies to come together.

Political parties help candidates run for office. It takes a lot of teamwork to run for office. A candidate has to raise money. This is called fundraising. Political parties also help create signs and **slogans**. Parties also look for new politicians. They can talk to new candidates. They explain what it's like to run for office. Candidates need help with fundraising. They also need help talking to voters. Political parties teach them what to do. It's important for people to vote. Political parties depend on voters. The parties place ads for candidates. They inform voters about the issues. This helps their candidates get more votes.

The first campaign posters were very detailed. They included drawings of the candidates that made them look noble and serious.

Political parties are local, state, and national. A party helps candidates in different ways. They can help a local candidate meet voters. This isn't possible for every national candidate. Political parties are important at a national level.

Every four years, there is a presidential election. Republicans and Democrats pick one candidate for president. This is one of the biggest jobs of a political party. The parties hold **primary elections**. Primary elections happen at all levels. National ones are usually large. There are many candidates to choose from.

Each party helps their candidates **campaign**. Candidates travel to different states. States hold elections. The winner is chosen as the presidential candidate. Each political party holds a big meeting every four years. It is called a convention. These happen at the end of the primary elections. They announce their presidential candidate at the meeting. They also talk about other issues. The party decides what ideas are most important to them. They share these ideas with the voters.

Voters don't have to join a political party. But some choose to join one. They vote in primary elections for their party. Some voters choose not to belong to a party. Voters do not have to vote for the same party in every election. They can pick the best candidate. Some voters choose candidates from both political parties. They can also switch political parties at any time.

CHAPTER 2

HISTORY OF THE REPUBLICAN PARTY

The Republican Party is one of the two major political parties in the United States. There is usually a Republican candidate in every election. The Republican Party is also known as the "GOP." That stands for "Grand Old Party." The nickname comes from the 1870s. It is also called the **conservative** party.

The word "Republican" was first used in US politics in 1792. Thomas Jefferson created what was then called the Democratic-Republican party. Jefferson did not want the **federal** government to have too much power. This is still a belief of the Republican Party.

THE GOP ELEPHANT

The Republican Party **logo** is the elephant. They took the symbol from cartoonist Thomas Nast. He drew the Democratic Party as a donkey in 1828. In the 1870s, he made the Republicans into an elephant. The elephant was standing strong against the Democratic donkey. Today, the elephant logo is used on many official Republican Party signs.

The elephant became the symbol of the Republican Party in 1874.

Cartoonist Thomas Nast drew a cartoon with a donkey scaring all of the animals in a zoo except the mighty elephant. The elephant stood for the strength of the Republican Party.

However, the Democratic-Republican Party grew into the Democratic Party. The modern-day Republican Party began in the 1850s. This marked an important era for the US government. There were many big issues facing the country. One issue was adding new states. Another issue was slavery. People disagreed about what to do. Should the United States get bigger? Should slavery continue?

The Kansas-Nebraska Act was suggested in 1854. The act allowed slavery in Kansas and Nebraska. They were new territories, or areas of land that were not yet states.

Many people did not want that to happen. They started a new political party. They said no slavery in Kansas and Nebraska. However, they did not push for the end of slavery in the southern states. This was the beginning of the Republican Party. Their first convention was held on July 6, 1854.

There have been 19 Republican presidents. This is the most of any political party. One of the most popular Republican presidents was Ronald Reagan. He served from 1981 to 1989. He was once a Democrat. But Reagan changed parties in 1964. Many Americans liked President Reagan. He won the most **electoral votes** in history. He also won 49 out of 50 states in his 1984 reelection. He was seen as a strong leader. His ideas were important to the Republican Party. He passed big tax cuts. President Reagan spent more money on the military. He picked three new judges for the Supreme Court. One was Sandra Day O'Connor. She was the first woman to serve on the Supreme Court. She was appointed in 1981.

Some Republican beliefs have been the same since the beginning of the party. One is states' rights. Republicans want states to have more power.

American people rushed to take their money out of the bank during the Great Depression. Many people lost everything they had during this time.

Other beliefs have changed over time. Many African Americans voted for the Republican Party after the Civil War. Republicans had opposed expanding slavery. African American support changed after the **Great Depression**. The Democrats passed a law called the **New Deal**. African American voters liked the idea. The Republican Party did not agree with it. They thought it made the government too big. They felt individual freedom was important. Many people switched political parties at this time.

The United States has had to face many challenges. Each political party has to decide on the best way to solve new problems. Today, the Republican Party is seen as the conservative party. Republicans believe in cutting taxes. They think the government should not control businesses. The Republican Party does not believe in lots of rules about the environment. They want to give companies more freedom. The Republican Party also believes in traditional values. Generally, traditional values are what people believed when the country was founded. Republicans support marriage between men and women. They believe in gun rights. They also support a strong border. The Republican Party believes in freedom for every person.

CHAPTER 3

HISTORY OF THE DEMOCRATIC PARTY

The Democratic Party is the other major party in the United States. There is usually a Democratic candidate running in each election. The Democrats are also known as the **liberal** party. The Democrats are the oldest political party in the United States. They were founded in 1828.

> **THE DEMOCRATIC DONKEY**
>
> The logo for the Democratic Party is a donkey. It was first used in 1828. Andrew Jackson was the Democratic candidate for president. His rivals nicknamed him after the donkey. President Jackson thought it was funny. He used it in his own campaign. It was also used in cartoons by Thomas Nast.

The Democratic Party was first called the Democratic-Republican Party. Thomas Jefferson became the third US president in 1801. He was followed by James Madison in 1809. James Monroe was president from 1817 to 1825. All of these presidents were part of the Democratic-Republican Party.

The donkey was first used to describe Democrat Andrew
Jackson because of his stubborn behavior.

The party could not agree on one candidate during the presidential election of 1824. The party split into two groups. Each group picked a candidate. One group later became known as the Democratic Party.

The Civil War started in 1861. This caused a disagreement in the Democratic Party. There were War Democrats and Peace Democrats. They had to answer an important question. Do we support the war or call for it to end? The War Democrats supported Abraham Lincoln. They were against slavery. The Peace Democrats wanted to allow slavery in the South. This would make the southern states happy. It would keep the country together. The Democrats split their support. Political parties often disagree about something before they come to an agreement. The Democrats eventually decided to be against slavery. This brought them together.

There have been 15 Democratic presidents in history. This includes the first African American president. His name is Barack Obama. He was president from 2009 to 2017. One of the most successful Democratic presidents was Franklin D. Roosevelt. He served for three terms from 1933 to 1945.

Franklin D. Roosevelt won all four of his presidential elections in landslide victories. This means most people voted for him.

He was elected for a fourth term, but he died shortly after it started. He became president in the middle of the Great Depression. This was a hard time for the United States. People did not have a lot of money. Many people lost jobs.

President Roosevelt made many new laws. He created the New Deal. It gave people jobs. It also created support for **labor unions**. Roosevelt's ideas took America out of the Depression. Some of his programs are still used. One is minimum wage. He also created social security. Social security helps people retire when they can no longer work.

The Democratic Party has changed over time. It was popular in the southern United States. This changed during the 1960s. The Democratic Party supported giving rights to people of every race, sex, and religion. These are called civil rights. Many in the South disagreed with the new laws. This changed the Democratic Party. They lost old members. They also gained new members. The new members liked the ideas. Some beliefs have been important to the Democratic Party for a long time. These beliefs include a strong government. The party stays strong by accepting new ideas while keeping some of the old.

The Democratic Party is seen as the liberal party. That means they want to see steady changes in how problems are solved. They believe in the government making laws about how businesses should be run. They want to use tax dollars on programs, such as social security.

Both Republicans and Democrats gather every four years to announce their candidates for the presidential election. Thousands of party members attend.

The Democratic Party believes the government should protect the environment. They also support **progressive** social issues. The Democratic Party supports LGBT+ rights. They also support civil rights for immigrants. The Democratic Party believes in gun control. They want the government to help people who don't have jobs and struggle to pay their bills. These are some of the big ideas that separate the two parties. Every voter gets to decide which party has the best ideas.

GLOSSARY

campaign (kam-PAYN) To campaign is to work toward a political goal.

candidates (KAN-di-detz) Candidates are people who run for office.

conservative (kun-ser-vuh-tiv) Those who are conservative believe in traditional practices and values.

electoral votes (i-LEK-ter-ul VOHTS) An electoral vote is a vote cast by a member of the electoral college. The electoral college the process by which someone is elected president. It is made up of 538 representatives from all 50 states. To be elected president, a candidate must receive 270 electoral votes

federal (FED-er-ul) The federal government is the national government. The president is the head of the federal government.

Great Depression (GRAYT duh-PRE-shun) The Great Depression was a time of low business activity in the united states that started in 1929 and lasted until the mid-1930s.

independent (in-di-PEN-dunt) An independent candidate is not associated with the democratic or republican parties.

labor unions (LAY-ber YOON-yenz) Labor unions are organizations who protect the rights and interests of workers.

liberal (LIB-er-ul) Those who are liberal believe in social and political change.

logo (LOH-goh) A logo is a picture that stands for a company or organization.

New Deal (NOO DEEL) The New Deal was a program crated by President Franklin Roosevelt. It provided jobs and helped the united states recover from the great depression.

primary elections (PRY-mayr-ee ee-LEK-shuns) Primary elections allow voters to pick candidates for the general, or main, election.

progressive (pruh-GRES-siv) Those who are progressive favor new or modern ideas in politics and education.

ratify (RA-ti-fy) To ratify is to make a document or agreement official by signing or voting for it.

slogans (SLOH-genz) Slogans are words or phrases that are easy to remember and are used by a group or business to attract attention.

TO LEARN MORE

IN THE LIBRARY

Bausum, Ann. *Our Country's Presidents: A Complete Encyclopedia of the U.S. Presidency*. Boone, Iowa: National Geographic Children's Books, 2017.

Frith, Alex, et al. *Politics for Beginners*. London: Usborne Publishing, 2018.

Ragone, Nick. *The Everything American Government Book: From The Constitution To Present-Day Elections, All You Need To Understand Our Democratic System*. Avon, Massachusetts: Adams Media, 2004.

ON THE WEB

Visit our website for links to learn more about political parties in the United States:

childsworld.com/links

Note to Parents, Teachers, and Librarians: We routinely verify our Web links to make sure they are safe and active sites. So encourage your readers to check them out!

INDEX

Anti-Federalists, 6

campaign, 8, 9, 16
candidates, 4, 7, 8, 9, 10, 16, 18, 21
civil rights, 20, 21
conservative, 10, 15

elections, 4, 9, 10, 13, 16, 18, 19, 21

Federalists, 6
Franklin, Benjamin, 7
fundraising, 7

Great Depression, 14, 15, 19

Jackson, Andrew, 5, 16, 17
Jefferson, Thomas, 10, 16

liberal, 16, 20
Lincoln, Abraham, 5, 18

New Deal, 15, 20

Obama, Barack, 18
O'Connor, Sandra Day, 13

Reagan, Ronald, 13
Roosevelt, Franklin D., 18, 19, 20

slogans, 7

ABOUT THE AUTHOR

M. Weber is a teacher and writer. She has written for both kids and adults and enjoys helping people of all ages learn new things. She has written about history, sports, and the environment. When she is not writing, she enjoys spending time with her family and browsing at her local bookstore. She lives in Minnesota.